A Child's First Book of POEMS

with pictures by CYNDY SZEKERES

Golden Press/New York
Western Publishing Company, Inc./Racine, Wisconsin

Acknowledgments

The publisher has made every effort to trace the ownership of all copyrighted material and to secure permission from the copyright owners. Any omissions or errors are inadvertent, and we will be pleased to make the necessary corrections in future printings.

"As Soon As It's Fall," "Feet," "Grasses," "The Handiest Nose," and "Like a Bug," from *Cricket in a Thicket* by Aileen Fisher. Copyright © 1963 by Aileen Fisher. Reprinted by permission of Atheneum Publishers. "Bedtime" and "Choosing," from *Eleanor Farjeon's Poems for Children.* Originally published in *Over the Garden Wall,* copyright 1933 by Eleanor Farjeon. Copyright renewed 1961. Reprinted by permission of J. B. Lippincott, Publishers, and Harold Ober Associates, Incorporated. "The Bullfrog's Song," reprinted with permission of Macmillan Publishing Co., Inc., from *Rings and Things* by Anita Posey. Copyright © 1967 by Anita Posey. "Cats," from *The Children's Bells* by Eleanor Farjeon. Reprinted by permission of David Higham Associates Limited. "The Elf and the Dormouse," reprinted by permission of Hawthorn Properties (Elsevier-Dutton Publishing Co., Inc.) from the book *Artful Antiks,* copyright 1922, 1950 by Oliver Herford. "Hiding," reprinted by permission of G. P. Putnam's Sons from *The Favorite Poems of Dorothy Aldis* by Dorothy Aldis. Copyright © 1970 by Roy E. Porter. "The Huntsmen," from *Rhymes and Verses: Collected Poems for Children* by Walter de la Mare. Reprinted by permission of the Literary Trustees of Walter de la Mare and The Society of Authors as their representative. "In the Rain," from *A Posy of Little Verses* by René Cloke. Reprinted by permission of The Hamlyn Publishing Group Limited. "The Light-house-keeper's White-Mouse," text from *I'll Read to You, You Read to Me* by John Ciardi. Copyright © 1962 by John Ciardi. Reprinted by permission of J. B. Lippincott, Publishers. "The Little Turtle," reprinted with permission of Macmillan Publishing Co., Inc. from *Collected Poems* by Vachel Lindsay. Copyright 1920 by Macmillan Publishing Co., Inc., renewed 1948 by Elizabeth C. Lindsay. "The Mare," reprinted with permission of Macmillan Publishing Co., Inc., and the British publishers, William Heinemann Ltd., from *Pillicock Hill* by Herbert Asquith (New York: Macmillan, 1926). "Mice," from *Fifty-one New Nursery Rhymes* by Rose Fyleman. Copyright 1931, 1932 by Doubleday & Company, Inc. Reprinted by permission of Doubleday & Company, Inc., and The Society of Authors, literary representative of the Estate of Rose Fyleman. "Mr. Rabbit," by Dixie Willson, from *Child Life* Magazine, copyright 1924, 1952 by Rand McNally & Company. Reprinted by permission of Dana W. Briggs. "My Puppy," from *Up the Windy Hill* by Aileen Fisher. Reprinted by permission of Scott, Foresman and Company. "Puppy and I," from *When We Were Very Young* by A. A. Milne. Copyright 1924 by E. P. Dutton & Co., Inc. Renewal, 1952, by A. A. Milne. Reprinted by permission of the publisher, E. P. Dutton; Associated Book Publishers for the British publishers, Methuen and Company Ltd.; and the Canadian Publishers, McClelland and Stewart Limited, Toronto. "Tea With Me," from *Roundabout* by Alison Winn. Reprinted by permission of Hodder & Stoughton Limited. "There Was Once a Puffin," by Florence Page Jaques, from *Child Life* Magazine, copyright 1930, 1958 by Rand McNally & Company. Reprinted by permission of The Nature Conservancy. "Wanted," by Rose Fyleman. Reprinted by permission of The Society of Authors, literary representative of the Estate of Rose Fyleman. "The Woodpecker," from *Under the Tree* by Elizabeth Madox Roberts. Copyright 1922 by B. W. Huebsch, Inc., copyright renewed 1950 by Ivor S. Roberts. Reprinted by permission of Viking Penguin, Inc.

 Library of Congress Catalog Card Number: 81-80484 ISBN 0-307-15812-8 ISBN 0-307-65812-0 (lib. bdg.)   DEFGHIJ

Contents

The Handiest Nose

An elephant's nose
is the handiest nose,
the handiest nose of all—
it curves and sways
in the cleverest ways,
and trumpets a bugle call;
it reaches high
in the leafy sky
for bunches of leaves to eat,
and snuffs around
all over the ground,
and dusts the elephant's feet.

An elephant's nose
is the dandiest nose,
the handiest nose of all
for holding a palm,
when the day is calm,
as an elephant's parasol,
and making a spray
for a sultry day,
and a hose for sprinkling, too,
and a hand to wag
near your peanut bag
when you watch him at the zoo.

Oh, an elephant's nose
is fun to see,
an elephant's nose is fine;
it's clever as ever
a nose can be
but I'm glad it isn't *mine*.

Aileen Fisher

The Little Turtle

There was a little turtle.
He lived in a box.
He swam in a puddle.
He climbed on the rocks.

He snapped at a mosquito.
He snapped at a flea.
He snapped at a minnow.
And he snapped at me.

He caught the mosquito.
He caught the flea.
He caught the minnow.
But he didn't catch me.

Vachel Lindsay

Like a Bug

Do you ever wonder
what it's like to be a bug,

Fitted in a jacket
that is stiff and rather snug.

Sleeping in a thistle
or beneath a leafy rug,

Never having gingersnaps
or cocoa in a mug,

Or a father you can talk to,
or a puppy you can hug?

Aileen Fisher

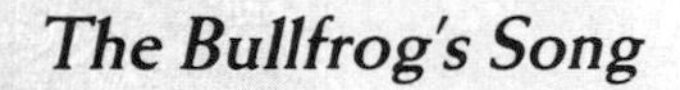

The Bullfrog's Song

The bullfrog sang the strangest song;
He sang it night and day.
"Ker-runk, ker-runk! Ker-runk, ker-runk!"
Was all it seemed to say.
A duck who liked to sing thought he
Would give the song a try;
"Ker-runk!" "Quack-Quack!"
"Ker-runk!" "Quack-Quack!"
They sang as I walked by.

The spotted cow had never heard
A more delightful song;
Right then and there, the spotted cow
Began to sing along.
The frog, the duck, the spotted cow
Sang out so loud and clear,
"Ker-runk!" "Quack-Quack!"
"Ker-runk!" "Moo-Moo!"
Was all that I could hear.

The speckled hen, a mother hen,
Whose work is never done,
Began to sing; for she knew when
You sing, your work is fun.
The frog, the duck, the cow, the hen,
All sang the happy song;
"Ker-runk!" "Quack-Quack!"
"Moo-Moo!" "Cluck-Cluck!"
They sang the whole day long.

Anita E. Posey

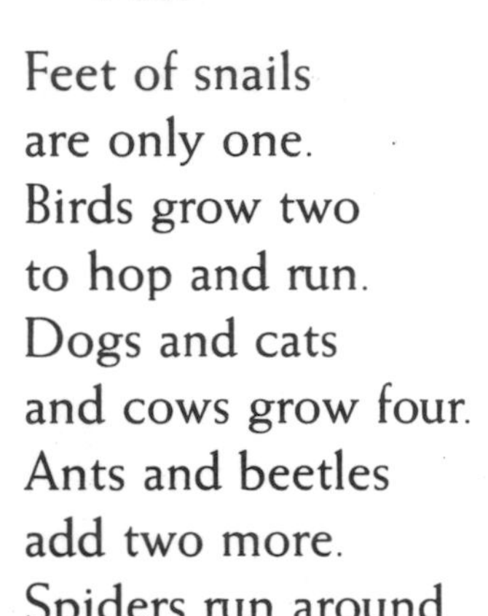

Feet

Feet of snails
are only one.
Birds grow two
to hop and run.
Dogs and cats
and cows grow four.
Ants and beetles
add two more.
Spiders run around
on eight,
which may seem
a lot, but wait—
Centipedes
have more than *thirty*
feet to wash
when they get dirty.

Aileen Fisher

Grasses

Do you ever wonder
if horses and such
like all grasses
equally much?

Or are some grasses
like spinach and prunes
and others like
coconut macaroons?

Aileen Fisher

Mr. Rabbit

Mr. Rabbit has a habit
That is very cute to see.

He wrinkles up and crinkles up
His little nose at me.

I like my little rabbit,
And I like his little brother,

And we have a lot of fun
Making faces at each other!

Dixie Willson

As Soon As It's Fall

Rabbits and foxes
as soon as it's fall
get coats that are warm
with no trouble at all,
coats that are furry
and woolly and new,
heavy and thick
so the cold can't get through.

They don't have to buy them
or dye them or try them,
they don't have to knit them
or weave them or fit them,
they don't have to sew them
or stitch them all through,

They just have to *grow* them,
and that's what they do.

Aileen Fisher

Tea With Me

A little brown bird looked in to see
What I was spreading on bread for tea.
He looked so hungry I felt I must
Eat the middle and leave him the crust.

The very next day he came again
Shivering cold in the pouring rain.
"I'm hungrier *still* today," he said.
So I ate the crusts and gave him the bread.

Now every day, whatever the weather,
That sparrow and I have our tea-time together.
We chirrup and chatter like very old friends
And I eat the odds up while he eats the ends.

Alison Winn

The Woodpecker

The woodpecker pecked out a little round hole
And made him a house in the telephone pole.
One day when I watched he poked out his head,
And he had on a hood and a collar of red.
When the streams of rain pour out of the sky,
And the sparkles of lightning go flashing by,
And the big, big wheels of thunder roll,
He can snuggle back in the telephone pole.

Elizabeth Madox Roberts

A Bird

A bird came down the walk:
He did not know I saw;
He bit an angleworm in halves
And ate the fellow, raw.

And then he drank a dew
From a convenient grass,
And then hopped sidewise to the wall
To let a beetle pass.

Emily Dickinson

There Was Once a Puffin

Oh, there once was a Puffin
Just the shape of a muffin,
And he lived on an island
In the
bright
blue sea!

He ate little fishes,
That were most delicious,
And he had them for supper
And he
had
them
for tea.

But this poor little Puffin,
He couldn't play nothin',
For he hadn't anybody
To
play
with
at all.

So he sat on his island,
And he cried for awhile, and
He felt very lonely,
And he
felt
very small.

Then along came the fishes,
And they said, "If you wishes,
You can have us for playmates,
Instead
of
for
tea!"

So they now play together,
In all sorts of weather,
And the puffin eats pancakes,
Like you
and
like
me.

Florence Page Jaques

My Puppy

It's funny
my puppy
knows just how I feel.

When I'm happy
he's yappy
and squirms like an eel.

When I'm grumpy
he's slumpy
and stays at my heel.

It's funny
my puppy
knows such a great deal.

Aileen Fisher

Puppy and I

I met a Man as I went walking;
We got talking,
Man and I.
"Where are you going to, Man?" I said
(I said to the Man as he went by).
"Down to the village to get some bread.
Will you come with me?" "No, not I."

I met a Horse as I went walking;
We got talking,
Horse and I.
"Where are you going to, Horse, today?"
(I said to the Horse as he went by).
"Down to the village to get some hay.
Will you come with me?" "No, not I."

I met a Woman as I went walking;
We got talking,
Woman and I.
"Where are you going to, Woman, so early?"
(I said to the Woman as she went by).
"Down to the village to get some barley.
Will you come with me?" "No, not I."

I met some Rabbits as I went walking;
We got talking,
Rabbits and I.
"Where are you going in your brown fur coats?"
(I said to the Rabbits as they went by).
"Down to the village to get some oats.
Will you come with us?" "No, not I."

I met a Puppy as I went walking;
We got talking,
Puppy and I.
"Where are you going this fine day?"
(I said to the Puppy as he went by).
"Up in the hills to roll and play."
"I'll come with you, Puppy," said I.

A. A. Milne

Wild Beasts

I will be a lion
And you shall be a bear,
And each of us will have a den
Beneath a nursery chair;
And you must growl and growl and growl,
And I will roar and roar,
And then—why, then—you'll growl again,
And I will roar some more!

Evaleen Stein

Choosing

Which will you have, a ball or a cake?
A cake is so nice, yes, that's what I'll take.

Which will you have, a cake or a cat?
A cat is so soft, I think I'll take that.

Which will you have, a cat or a rose?
A rose is so sweet, I'll have that, I suppose.

Which will you have, a rose or a book?
A book full of pictures?—oh, do let me look!

Which will you have, a book or a ball?
Oh, a ball! No, a book! No, a—
There! have them all!

Eleanor Farjeon

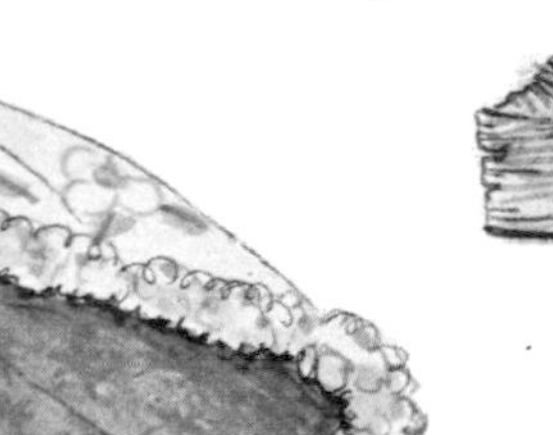

New Shoes

When I am walking down the street
I do so like to watch my feet.
Perhaps you do not know the news,
Mother has bought me fine new shoes!
When the left one steps I do not speak,
I listen to its happy squeak.

Marjorie Seymour Watts

Hiding

I'm hiding, I'm hiding,
And no one knows where,
For all they can see is my
Toes and my hair.

And I just heard my father
Say to my mother,
"But, darling, he must be
Somewhere or other;

Have you looked in the inkwell?"
And Mother said, "Where?"
"In the inkwell," said Father. But
I was not there.

Then "Wait!" cried my mother.
"I think that I see
Him under the carpet." But
It was not me.

"Inside the mirror's
A pretty good place,"
Said Father and looked, but saw
Only his face.

"We've hunted," sighed Mother,
"As hard as we could,
And I am so afraid that we've
Lost him for good."

Then I laughed out aloud,
And I wiggled my toes,
And Father said, "Look, dear,
I wonder if those

Toes could be Benny's.
There are ten of them. See?"
And they were so surprised to find
Out it was me!

Dorothy Aldis

The Swing

How do you like to go up in a swing,
  Up in the air so blue?
Oh, I do think it the pleasantest thing
  Ever a child can do!

Up in the air and over the wall,
  Till I can see so wide,
Rivers and trees and cattle and all
  Over the countryside—

Till I look down on the garden green,
  Down on the roof so brown—
Up in the air I go flying again,
  Up in the air and down!

Robert Louis Stevenson

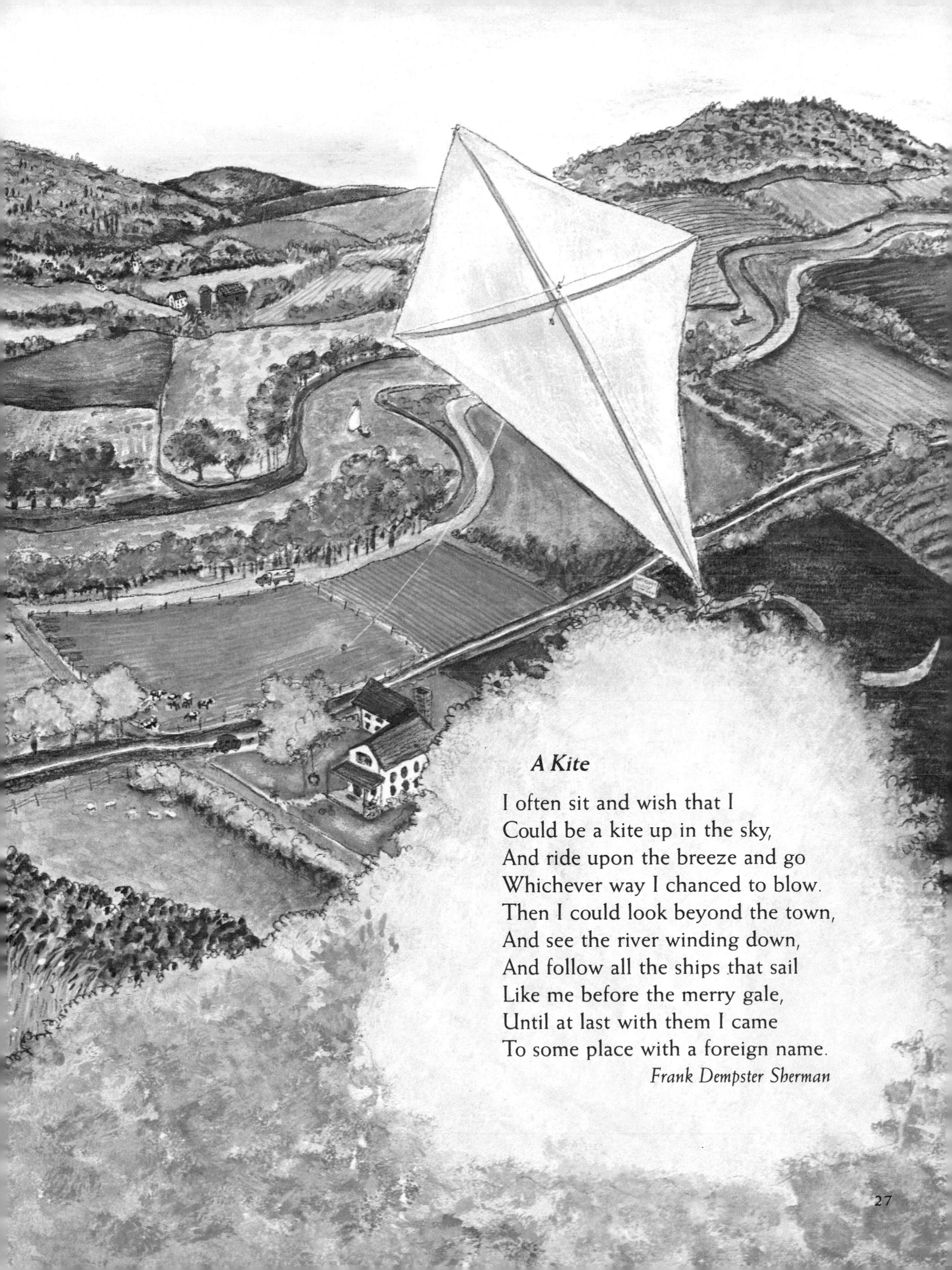

A Kite

I often sit and wish that I
Could be a kite up in the sky,
And ride upon the breeze and go
Whichever way I chanced to blow.
Then I could look beyond the town,
And see the river winding down,
And follow all the ships that sail
Like me before the merry gale,
Until at last with them I came
To some place with a foreign name.

Frank Dempster Sherman

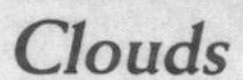

Clouds

White sheep, white sheep,
On a blue hill,
When the wind stops
You all stand still.
When the wind blows
You walk away slow.
White sheep, white sheep,
Where do you go?

Christina Rossetti

Who Has Seen the Wind?

Who has seen the wind?
    Neither I nor you;
But when the leaves hang trembling,
    The wind is passing through.

Who has seen the wind?
    Neither you nor I:
But when the trees bow down their heads,
    The wind is passing by.

Christina Rossetti

Rain

The rain is raining all around,
It falls on field and tree;
It rains on the umbrellas here,
And on the ships at sea.

Robert Louis Stevenson

In the Rain

There is no color in the rain
It's only water, wet and plain.
It makes damp spots upon my book
And splashes on my new dress, look!
But puddles, in the rainy weather,
Glisten like a peacock's feather.

René Cloke

The Elf and the Dormouse

Under a toadstool crept a wee Elf,
Out of the rain, to shelter himself.

Under the toadstool, sound asleep,
Sat a big Dormouse all in a heap.

Trembled the wee Elf, frightened, and yet
Fearing to fly away lest he get wet.

To the next shelter—maybe a mile!
Sudden the wee Elf smiled a wee smile,

Tugged till the toadstool toppled in two,
Holding it over him, gayly he flew.

Soon he was safe home, dry as could be,
Soon woke the Dormouse—"Good gracious me!

Where is my toadstool?" loud he lamented.
And that's how umbrellas first were invented.

Oliver Herford

The Light-house-keeper's White-Mouse

As I rowed out to the light-house
For a cup of tea one day,
I came upon a very wet white-mouse
Out swimming in the bay.

"If you are for the light-house,"
Said he, "I'm glad we met.
I'm the light-house-keeper's white-mouse
And I fear I'm getting wet."

"O light-house-keeper's white-mouse,
I am rowing out for tea
With the keeper in his light-house.
Let me pull you in with me."

So I gave an oar to the white-mouse.
And I pulled on the other.
And we all had tea at the light-house
With the keeper and his mother.

John Ciardi

The City Mouse and the Garden Mouse

The city mouse lives in a house;
The garden mouse lives in a bower,
He's friendly with the frogs and toads,
And sees the pretty plants in flower.

The city mouse eats bread and cheese;
The garden mouse eats what he can;
We will not grudge him seeds and stocks,
Poor little timid furry man.

Christina Rossetti

Mice

I think mice
Are rather nice.

Their tails are long,
Their faces small,
They haven't any
Chins at all.
Their ears are pink,
Their teeth are white,
They run about
The house at night.
They nibble things
They shouldn't touch
And no one seems
To like them much.

But *I* think mice
Are nice.

Rose Fyleman

Wanted

I'm looking for a house
Said the little brown mouse,
with
One room for breakfast,
One room for tea,
One room for supper,
And that makes three.

One room to dance in,
When I give a ball,
A kitchen and a bedroom,
Six rooms in all.

Rose Fyleman

The Chickens

Said the first little chicken,
With a queer little squirm,
"I wish I could find
A fat little worm!"

Said the next little chicken,
With an odd little shrug:
"I wish I could find
A fat little bug!"

Said the third little chicken,
With a small sigh of grief:
"I wish I could find
A green little leaf!"

Said the fourth little chicken,
With a faint little moan:
"I wish I could find
A wee gravel stone!"

"Now see here!" said the mother,
From the green garden patch,
"If you want any breakfast,
Just come here and scratch!"

Anonymous

The Barnyard

When the Farmer's day is done,
In the barnyard, every one,
Beast and bird politely say,
"Thank you for my food to-day."

The cow says, "Moo!"
The pigeon, "Coo!"
The sheep says, "Baa!"
The lamb says, "Maa!"
The hen, "Cluck! Cluck!"
"Quack!" says the duck;
The dog, "Bow Wow!"

The cat, "Meow!"
The horse says, "Neigh!
I love sweet hay!"
The pig near by,
Grunts in his sty.

When the barn is locked up tight,
Then the farmer says, "Good-night!"
Thanks his animals, every one,
For the work that has been done.

Maud Burnham

Cats

Cats sleep
Anywhere,
Any table,
Any chair,
Top of piano,
Window-ledge,
In the middle,
On the edge,
Open drawer,
Empty shoe,
Anybody's
Lap will do,
Fitted in a
Cardboard box,
In the cupboard
With your frocks—
Anywhere!
They don't care!
Cats sleep
Anywhere.

Eleanor Farjeon

The Mare

Look at the mare of Farmer Giles!
She's brushing her hooves on the mat;

Look at the mare of Farmer Giles!
She's knocked on the door, rat-a-tat!

With a clack of her hoof and a wave of her head
She's tucked herself up in the four-post bed,
And she's wearing the Farmer's hat!

Herbert Asquith

The Huntsmen

Three jolly gentlemen,
In coats of red,
Rode their horses
Up to bed.

Three jolly gentlemen
Snored till morn,
Their horses champing
The golden corn.

Three jolly gentlemen,
At break of day,
Came clitter-clatter down the stairs
And galloped away.

Walter de la Mare

Bedtime

Five minutes, five minutes more, please!
Let me stay five minutes more!
Can't I just finish the castle
I'm building here on the floor?
Can't I just finish the story
I'm reading here in my book?
Can't I just finish this bead-chain—
It *almost* is finished, look!
Can't I just finish this game, please?
When a game's once begun
It's a pity never to find out
Whether you've lost or won.
Can't I just stay five minutes?
Well, can't I stay just four?
Three minutes, then? two minutes?
Can't I stay *one* minute more?

Eleanor Farjeon

The Moon

I see the moon,
And the moon sees me;
God bless the moon,
And God bless me.

Anonymous